THE COAST OF OREGON

THE COAST OF OREGON

Photography by
MICHAEL BREUER

◆

Introduction by
PETER JENSEN

SKYLINE
PRESS

Produced by Boulton Publishing Services Inc., Toronto
Designed by Fortunato Aglialoro

©1985 Oxford University Press (Canadian Branch)
SKYLINE PRESS is a registered imprint of the Oxford University Press

ISBN 0-19-540627-3
1 2 3 4 – 8 7 6 5
Printed in Hong Kong by Scanner Art Services, Inc., Toronto

All images for this book were taken
with Leica cameras and Leitz lenses,
focal lengths from 21mm to 400mm.

INTRODUCTION

In terms of ruggedness, few coastlines match Oregon's battered brow. The waves push unimpeded across 6,000 miles of ocean in a headlong assault, their nibbling crests equal in height to a two-storey building, striking basaltic rock with the force of a thousand logging trucks. The land gives, falls back, surrenders—but slowly—to ceaseless abrasion and thunderous uppercuts that send water and air whistling through rock cracks like an explosive fuel mixture in a compressing cylinder. Logs, stripped of their bark by rivers and waves, float seaward at high tide only to be hurled ashore again.

The ocean is a restless creature, caged by shorelines, throwing its bones against the bars.

The land seems to have always been here, accepting punishment through countless millennia. Geologic evidence, however, suggests that these rocky shores may have drifted across the earth's surface from a global sector that is now Japan and China. Oregon is a mix of alien continental fragments, 'terranes', swept up as the globe wrinkled and stretched its thin skin.

Inland from broken seacoast edges, Oregon rises in a coastal range that shields the fertile Willamette River Valley from the sea's capriciousness. Rivers cut deep through heavily wooded ramparts, then stretch and curve along coastal valleys on their way to the surf. In heavy rains, which occur with drenching regularity, river and creek mouths bleed a turbulent burden of silt across their bars into the open sea. Returning to the shore as sand, the grains are just another weapon in the assault.

It is at once a hostile and a friendly shore. Indians camped for generations at the river mouths, walking the forest paths, eating herring eggs and clams from the lagoons, trapping the big salmon headed upstream to spawn. They noted the daily changes in the beach as a broker watches the Dow Jones board; a layer of soft, fluffy sand laid over grains packed firm and hard meant that waves were building the beach. Razorback clams, equipped with strong digging feet, would be harder to reach. In a few days, the shore could change from a quarry site of large cobbles and multicolored, marble-size stones, into a fine-grained, dark-green blanket of basaltic grains.

The first boats of foreigners may have been seen as early as the fifth century (when Liang Dynasty court records show that Chinese explorer Hwui Shan sailed to the eastern Pacific rim). Traders at the helms of huge, bat-winged junks probed the shore for unusual minerals and animal life. Iron tools from the fifteenth century have been unearthed at the Alava dig in Washington, and the same traders probably visited the mouth of the Columbia River, site of many Indian villages. A century or more later, Sir Francis Drake, his tiny caravel *Golden Hind* fresh from a careening somewhere in central California, sailed past hurriedly in 1579 on his quest for a Northwest Passage, naming the coast New Albion.

The Indian era gave way slowly in the eighteenth and early nineteenth centuries. A Russian expedition led by Vitus Bering chronicled the coast's potential treasure of furs: seals, sea lions, beavers, and—most desirable of all—playful sea otters. The small animals floated in offshore kelp beds by the hundreds of thousands, lazing on their backs, or diving for mollusks which they cracked open with a rock plucked from the bottom. Soon the *promyshleniki* (Russian fur hunters) seemed bent on clothing the entire aristocracy of Peter the Great's Russia in thick, warm, otter fur. Not far behind were the Europeans and Americans. Captain James Cook on *Resolution*'s last voyage in 1788 journaled: 'the fur of these animals is certainly softer and finer than that of any others we know of, and therefore, the discovery of this part of the continent of North America where so valuable an article of commerce may be met with, cannot be a matter of indifference.' Captain William Clark of the Lewis and Clark overland expedition (the first Americans to reach the Pacific Northwest by land) added, on meeting a party of Chinooks, '…one of the Indians had on a robe made of two sea otter Skins, the fur of them were more beautiful than any fur I had ever seen.' The Indians did not turn over their rich hunting grounds and timberlands without frequent skirmishes (and not a few massacres on both sides), but the tide of exploration and settlement seemed never to ebb after these first encounters.

A coastline that had nurtured the Indians for so many centuries, providing them with abundant food and shelter, began to challenge a new inhabitant. It was not immediately embraced by the newcomers as a pleasant place. When Lewis and Clark reached the mouth of the Columbia River (Oregon's northern state line) their journals proclaimed 'Great joy in camp. We are in view of the ocean, this great Pacific Ocean which we have been so long anxious to see. The roaring or noise made by the waves breaking on the rocky shores (as I suppose) may be heard distinctly.'

Joy soon turned to despair at the wet, challenging conditions of a winter on the Oregon coast. Forced at first to camp on an immense pile of drift-logs and wood near the

Columbia's mouth, the party enjoyed an afternoon diversion when the flood tide came in (to paraphrase Clark) 'accompanied with immense waves and heavy winds, floated the trees and drift which was on the point on which we camped, and tossed them about in such a manner as to endanger the canoes very much. Every exertion and the strictest attention by every individual of the party was scarcely sufficient to save our canoes from being crushed by those monstrous trees, many of them nearly 200 feet long and from four to seven feet through. Our camp was entirely under water during the height of the tide, every man as wet as water could make them all the last night and today all day as the rain continued all day...' Eventually the party built Fort Clatsop near the Columbia River mouth and weathered a winter that brought barely a week of sunshine. Its temporary log walls had crumbled into a rotten pile by the time the first white settlers arrived on the Clatsop Plains.

Oregon's first city, Astoria, rose near Clatsop as settlers began to draw their livelihood off the sea, river, forests, and rich bottom-land in the river valleys. Fishermen took to the sea across the infamous Columbia River bar, where waves as high as 25 feet were not uncommon, or trolled upriver for migrating salmon. Astoria's grandest house, the Flavel Mansion, was built by Captain George Flavel, one of the first bar pilots licensed by the Oregon Territory in 1852.

The merciless hunt for otter continued. On shore, farmers flocked to the virtues of the inland Willamette Valley, but coastal valleys also gave rich yields and families migrated southward along the coast from Astoria. Beaches were used in early days as roadways until narrow tracks could be cut into steep, forested headlands. Small settlements grew beside mirror-smooth lagoons or at the mouths of coastal rivers whose Indian names sounded like gentle incantations— Siltcoos, Nehalem, Siuslaw, Yaquina, Nestucca, Umpqua.

It was a history of quiet growth, punctuated by the twisting, *whooshing* falls of giant trees in the forests and much later the sputter of diesel engines in the fishing boats. The wilderness coast has endured man, allowing incursions, but never succumbing to any outright takeover other than an occasional blur of neon light above a curio shop. Is it such a great distance from a Lewis and Clark scout trading his blue beads for otter skins, to a shopkeeper in Lincoln City offering tourists brightly colored postcards and agates?

My earliest memories of the Oregon coast include great plumes of surf, barking sea lions, and mists tethered to offshore 'haystack' rock formations. But it is a cryptic snatch of dialogue that first comes to mind:

'This is the place, Pebble Pup!'

'Yup!'

I was introduced to the Oregon coast in the back seat of our family station wagon, when I was barely old enough to see over the door panel as the Highway 101 tableau rolled by. We stopped often; even a quarter century ago the coastal route was renowned as one of the most beautiful drives in the world, and there were constant diversions, including over 30 state parks and dozens of oddly named towns pressed between the sudden coastal range and the advancing Pacific. In one town, emblazoned on a tourist rock-shop above the crudely painted caricatures of a prospector and his dog 'Pebble Pup', floated my now-favorite line of Oregon coast dialogue. Pithy, like Oregonians. Homey. Why would a pup need say more than 'Yup'?

Inside I let polished agates gleaned from the beach run through my fingers, clicking back into their bins like hard, clear, vitamin capsules. My father allowed me to buy five small stones, and they nestled in the bottom of my jeans' pocket for the rest of the journey.

We followed the shoreline for a week. Bridges arched over mountain freshets born only a few miles back from the surf, or collared greater rivers, one with the wonderful name 'Rogue'. Sand dunes, pushed inland by waves and wind, swallowed pines and telephone poles in shifting flows. Wilderness seemed always at the roadside, tempting my younger sister and I to lean too far into a blackberry bramble and come up scratched and bleeding, but with lips stained a satisfying purple, or to wander a narrow trail through the gray, rasping grass down to a hidden beach.

Coursing through each day, almost always in earshot, was the surf. Big surf hitting the rocks with hollow, jarring cannon shots. Hissing at the cobbled beaches. Bearding the rocks with froth. The Pacific never did live up to its name.

In a town called Gold Beach we left our car for a day to board the Rogue River jet boats. Often called 'mail boats', they cruised upriver over 30 miles to the lodges at Agness. As the river narrowed between gray bookends of rock a sudden hollow *craack* sounded beneath our feet, and a mushroom of clear, cold water pushed up through the floorboards. Quickly our pilot steered us to the eddying shallows, where the long, flat-keeled boat settled into about four feet of water. I remember my father picking up one small splintered piece of the hull as we waded ashore. It hung for years on our kitchen bulletin board, inscribed with the words 'The Great Rogue River Shipwreck. All Hands Saved!'

Over the years Oregon's coastal highway has rolled

beneath me many times. My wife and I (and now our small children) return whenever we can to the map's thin red line marked '101'. The lighthouses, standing like quarterbacks in a surge of onrushing linemen, continue to hold my family's fascination, gathering local lore to their lenses as the years, and storms, go by. Of all the lighthouses, one on Tillamook Rock (several miles out to sea) has the most stories to tell about the Oregon ocean's power. Here a monster wave once tossed a rock weighing 135 pounds higher than the light, which is almost 140 feet above normal sea level. How do we know the rock's weight today? It crashed through the lightkeeper's cottage roof. On another occasion, a lightkeeper checked a malfunctioning foghorn 95 feet above the sea and found it chocked with rocks.

There have been moments of solitary euphoria, such as the time I played the Salishan golf course alone in a blowing, early morning rain rather than drive on to our next night's lodgings, holding my wet clubs by wrapping a handkerchief around the leather grips, smelling the salt spray coming over the dunes and the low roofs of beautiful seashore homes. At one tee I stopped to breakfast on the ubiquitous blackberries while a buck deer picked his way through the lush groundcover just a chip shot away.

Smoked salmon wrapped in wax paper… A summer play in a barnlike building in Cannon Beach… Great blocks of curdy cheddar cheese being cut and flipped in a Tillamook factory… Hours spent walking the beach, climbing the whirls of driftwood stumps piled against the cliffs… Photographing a bridge framing a sunset while a line of pelicans skims the waves. All this is Oregon.

All this is *the place*. Ain't that right, Pebble Pup?

PETER JENSEN

1 Tillamook Bay, not far from the famous cheese-making region. Locals call this 'the land of cheese, trees, and ocean breeze.' In 1788 the American ship *Lady Washington* anchored here while the scurvied crew went ashore to search for fruit.

2 *(left)* Banded by waves hitting the rocky reefs at low tide, the coastline south of Devil's Punchbowl makes a great curve near Cape Foulweather.

3 Heceta Head Lighthouse, built in 1894, punctuates a basaltic-rock promontory above Devil's Elbow State Park beach.

4 Heading inland from Yachats, springtime travelers find country lanes lined with flowering fruit trees. The Indian word Yachats (pronounced Ya-hots) means 'at the base of the mountain.'

5 (right) Sheep graze the rolling hill country. Early settlers, constantly confronted with low mountains and valleys like this open region near Carpenterville, often used the beaches as 'highways' at low tide.

6 White on white: Allegany Church, east of Coos Bay, dressed in spring finery.

7 *(right)* Moist, shady woods of the coastal ranges bear carpets of wildflowers. Here buttercups nod toward the sunlight in Siuslaw National Forest, north of Otis.

8 *(left)* Harbor seal near Strawberry Hill. Harbor seals often fish the Oregon estuaries, following the tidal flow.

9 Ancient 'haystack' rock rises like a tooth from the beach south of Cape Blanco. Dead forests of driftwood wait for high tides and storms to float their numbers again to wreak havoc on the coast.

10 *(left)* Trillium, a member of the lily family, grows along streambanks and in deep woods of the Siuslaw Forest.

11 Classic Western barn, with its high hay loft and wing-like roofs, sits low in a valley north of Otis near Lincoln City.

12 *(left)* Wide-beamed *Ah So* sets to sea on a calm day at
Cape Kiwanda, steadied by her hip-booted crew. Most of
the town's boats are surf launched; many are sturdy
dories especially suited to braving the waves.

13 Cloud-swept sunset over Tillamook Bay.

14 *(left)* Dunes near Siltcoos Lake and Florence anchored by hip-high grasses.

15 Oldest lighthouse in Oregon, the Cape Blanco light rose in 1870 on the state's most westerly point, named for its chalky white appearance. This is an excellent place to sight migrating gray whales as they 'cut the corner' close to the Cape.

16 Beaches from south of Cape Sebastian all the way to Brookings are among the state's most scenic; wild, driftwood-tumbled places, close to the California border.

17 *(right)* Gulls at Moolack Beach like calligraphy in the sky, near Old Yaquina Bay Lighthouse, built in 1871.

18 Even the mighty Fresnel lens of a lighthouse can be dimmed by the thick fogs that often wrap the headlands. Heceta Head light winks here in vain.

19 (right) Advancing storm clouds near Seaside move in for a night of rain.

20 *(left)* An ancient lagoon caught by shifting sands and wind-pushed waves that barred exit to the sea, Cleawox Lake in Honeyman State Park serenely reflects its guardian dunes. The park is one of Oregon's most popular.

21 The sea south of Cape Lookout breaks into surflines that stretch out a quarter mile or more.

22 Graceful, mature Pacific madrona grow tall and straight in Hunter Creek Valley, east of Gold Beach.

23 *(right)* Garibaldi's Coast Guard station has a 'widow's walk' set high on its roof. The port here is a popular charter and whale-watching center.

24 Cape Arago Lighthouse sits on a sheer coastline above Bastendorf County Park—a fine beach for combing and picnicking.

25 *(right)* Exploding waves gradually fissure the rocks.

26 *(left)* Bridal-veil effect of Silver Falls in Golden and Silver Falls Park east of Coos Bay.

26 *(above)* Spilling off a pulpit of rock, Golden Falls, in Golden and Silver Falls Park.

27 *(right)* Skunk cabbage in a Tillamook bog.

28 Clarkias along the slopes south of Humbug Mountain.

29 *(right)* As if from a Bronte novel, historic Hughes House in Cape Blanco wraps itself in mists and windblown trees.

30 High and dry on a wharf in Port Orford, stubby fishing boats get a bottom scraping and new antifouling paint.

31 Beacon in a boneyard; Bullard Beach and its lighthouse.

32 *(left)* Siuslaw Forest surrounds Cape Perpetua, with its mist-lined vistas, quiet forest paths, and stately trees.

33 Branch patterns, Ecola State Park forest.

34 Trolling booms at attention, fishing boats bunch in Charleston harbor berths.

35 *(right)* Nets drape over Volkswagen-sized drum winches on trawlers' wide sterns.

36 *(left)* Crescent beach near Bandon, its waves slowed somewhat by offshore rocks, has built up an enormously wide shelf of sand.

37 Apocalyptic sea of foam greets the shore just south of Strawberry Hill.

38 *(left)* Quiet stretch of the Rogue River, where a great bar of sand has built up in the river's elbow.

39 Only a few trees cling to this rugged slope above Hunter Creek Valley.

40 Heaps of line, crab traps, and floats on *Stormy*'s stern, Coos Bay.

41 *(right)* Crumbling concrete of Fort Stevens State Park was first poured in 1863 to protect the mouth of the Columbia River from Confederates. The fort was fired upon by a Japanese submarine during World War II.

42 Twin sister architecturally of the Garibaldi Coast Guard station, Hammond's biological research station is an antique that yet houses modern research.

43 Astoria, called 'The Williamsburg of the West' is rich in parks, historic monuments, and venerable houses.

44 Rhododendron blossoms atop their moss-flecked stems in Honeyman State Park.

45 *(right)* A curve near Carpenterville shows through the trees as 101 makes the long Oregon journey from Washington to California.

46 *(left)* Crop of barnacle-like floats hangs from the stern of a Coos Bay boat in Port Orford.

47 Sawmill-bound raft of cut and trimmed logs gets a nudge from a Coos Bay tugboat.

48 Looking southward; surf lines below Cape Lookout.

49 *(right)* Steady winds and plenty of waves attract hearty windsurfers in Nehalem Bay.

50 Gravestones stitch the lawn of Gray Memorial Chapel, site of the first
American pioneer church west of the Rockies, south of Astoria.

51 Gray's Presbyterian congregation answered the call of this bell.

52 Tillamook's byways blaze with fall color.

53 *(right)* Restored botanical gardens in Shore Acres State Park, Sunset Bay, surround the original house with its odd little windows close up under the eaves.

54 A low garden of grasses and wildflowers near Yachats.

55 *(right)* Still day in Florence Harbor, when sky and water become one.

56 Deeply cut Devil's Lake fork of the Wilson River, east of Tillamook.

57 *(right)* 'Haystack' snags a cloud formation at sunset off Cape Kiwanda.

58 Flavel House, built for a sea captain, made restrained use of Victorian ornamentation. Flavel could watch his boats on the Columbia River from the upper stories.

59 Stout Umpqua Lighthouse, Winchester
Bay, shows its nineteenth century styling.
The keeper's tiny cottage clings like a foot to
the tower.

60 Cut off from land, rocky coastal fragments are eventually surrounded and undercut by waves. Harris State Park is inside the city limits of Brookings, a city famous for the cultivation of the Easter lily.

61 *(right)* The *Peter Iredale*, a four-masted British ship, still raises some of its battered timbers above the beach at Fort Stevens State Park, Astoria.

62 Few anchorages in the world challenged ship captains as did the Columbia River Bar. Astoria's maritime museum recalls the days of sail.

63 *(right)* The lightship *Columbia* now rests at anchor in Astoria after decades of hazardous duty.

64 *(left)* Sunset sky south of Florence.

65 Rock formations, Harris Beach State Park, Brookings.

66 *(left)* Lone Ranch Creek takes on the appearance of a
Japanese brush painting. One thin scarp marks the path of
fresh water to salt.

67 Sun burns through fog near Carpenterville.

68 Graceful bounds of Newport Harbor's bridge stretch across Yaquina Bay.

69 Coast Guard rescue boat, designed to take on heavy surf, in front of a
classic Coast Guard station in Newport.

70 (left) Common foxgloves spike the hillsides above 101 near Carpenterville.

71 Fluted, drooping foxglove blooms cling like snapdragons to their thick stalks.

72 Storm surf in Boiler Bay. Water levels can rise 15 feet or more along the shore; there simply isn't enough time for surf driven ashore to drain off before the next wave hits.

73 *(right)* Seal Rock fishermen stay high atop a shoreline rock, always watching for 'rogue' waves that might sweep them into the maelstrom.

74 Azaleas bloom wild near the mouth of the Chetco River in Brookings,
a fine stream for steelhead and salmon near the Rogue River.

75 *(right)* Near Florence is a coastal 'sahara', often peaceful, sometimes
alive with dune buggies crawling to the tops of the 250 ft high dunes.

76 *(left)* Surf play: a windsurfer, wetsuited against water temperatures in the '50s, jumps the tiny waves in Nehalem Bay.

77 Needle-sharp bill ready for small crabs and frogs, a heron stalks the shallows of Tillamook Bay.

78 Fleecy clouds and mists roll across the hillsides at Carpenterville.

79 *(right)* Rocky Mountain iris spreads atop a bluff above Cape Blanco 'haystack' rock.

80 Sunset near Cape Arago.

81 *(right)* Tillamook bay under cloud cover.

82 *(left)* Cold air drains to the valleys in Cape Perpetua forest, then warms up with first daylight.

83 Wave-cut sand ledges near Strawberry Hill south of Cape Perpetua. Waves can sometimes bite as much as five feet off a beach in one night of high tides and storm surf.

84 Yaquina lighthouse north of Newport, its lens like a fire in the mouth of a cannon.

85 *(right)* Sand dunes at Florence engulf the trees.

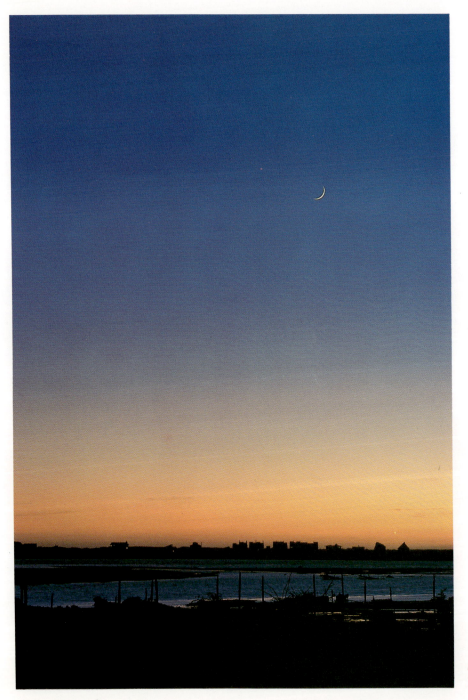

86 Moonrise over Lincoln Beach and Siletz River.